Sadness flies on the wings of morning and
out of the darkness comes the light. **"**
Anon

Tallulah Rendall

The Banshee And The Moon

Run Let The River Run

Canary

Pieces

She Rises Up

Shine On

Go My Way

Hear Me Now

The Banshee

Land Away

Trust In Me

Eyes

Lost In The Moonlight

Introduction

My first record, Libellus, took two years to record as I struggled to find direction. My second, Alive, was recorded live in just five days at Hookend Studios, in Oxfordshire, and captured the sound of my band. For this my third album, I wanted to focus on my essence as an artist and the energy of my live performances.

In August 2012 after the release of Alive, on my label Transducer Records, I was still struggling as an artist in the UK and so I turned my attention to Berlin. Soon after I headed out to play a ten-day tour, at the end of which I missed my return flight. I have never missed a flight. I took this as fate and at that moment decided to move cities and spend the next three months hibernating and writing in a flat in Prenzlau berg. Even though I am fiercely proud of my first two albums, it felt as though it was time to embrace who I was as an artist on my own, without any other creative influence, and so because of this, I spent hours alone playing bass, piano, writing harmonies and narrating stories.

It was a lonely time and the cold winds and low mists that give the Berlin streets an almost Dickensian feel meant that I was often drawn into the surreal. I didn't sleep well, woken often by haunting sounds of classical music echoing from the rooms below. But I was deeply inspired and by December 2012 I had written much of this record and I had found my muse: The Banshee. I had dreamt of this character, a wild woman: wise, free, powerful, honest and untameable. Reminiscent of Lady Godiva on her white steed, roaming across the heavens observing the world below and as I began to write her story I also became acutely aware of how far I felt I was from personally embodying her qualities. I was at a low ebb and the nocturnal Berlin life was not helping, but I was aware of a strength growing within.

During the previous summer I had become drawn to Qi Gong, and through retreats and classes had introduced a daily practice into my life. And so whilst surrounded by much uncertainty I focused time each day on what I knew was good for me. The result was an ever-growing clarity and determination to break many destructive patterns. This combined with a clear intention of what Banshee elements I did want present in my life inevitably led me to making a series of seemingly drastic decisions.

The first of these was inspired by a brief visit to the UK for Christmas. At a small gathering over New Year's I met Ben. He had been living in the Himalayas for the past twelve years working as an Ethnobotanist;

a world that couldn't have been further removed from my own, but whilst our external realities where seemingly incompatible our personalities and passions weren't and it was clear that we shone in each others presence. After three days of laughter and shared stories by firelight we returned to our different countries safe in the knowledge that a beautiful friendship had begun. Two months later and that friendship had developed into hour-long daily conversations over Skype and so embracing the impractical nature of it all Ben invited me to visit him. Never previously having had a desire to travel to India, for fear of illness and just the impracticality of being a blonde travelling alone, I was momentarily hesitant. That combined with the fact that I had previously only met Ben for three days made the decision a little daunting. However, my intuition was telling me to go. I had no gigs lined up and had yet to find a new home in Berlin so now was as good a time as ever to take a leap of faith and so I did. We spent three weeks travelling, exploring the Thar Desert in Rajasthan before heading up into the snowy landscape of the Himalayas to Ben's home where I wrote Go My Way and Run Let The River Run.

Upon returning to Germany, it was clear that my heart was still ensconced in the Himalayas. I had found a flat in Berlin though and was due to rent it for a year.

But whilst I had arrived in Germany, my worldly possessions hadn't. And for three weeks they failed to appear. Once again I was sure the Universe was intervening. And as I sat in the flat I was due to live in for the next year I decided this wasn't right. Ben, still in India, was faced with similar questions and so before long the decision was made: we would both return to England to live in a small cottage outside Bristol but first I would re-release my second album Alive, in Germany followed by a tour to promote it, whilst Ben packed up twelve years of Himalayan life.

For the release of Alive we took over a warehouse space and in one room created an art exhibition where each song from the record was represented by an installation, inspired by the original artwork. In the next room I performed backed by my German band with Lucas Dietrich on bass and Dan Telander on drums. This was to be followed by a tour of Germany. Disappointingly though the tour fell through and there were only a scattering of dates booked to promote the record. There were also problems developing between myself and the German label and the label and the PR Company, which unfortunately had a negative impact on the release. I had also just been dropped by my UK Publishing Label, which meant I would have no finances to record a third album.

Photograph by Paris Ackrill

On the positive side though I met Danton Supple. Danton is a highly acclaimed producer and engineer who has worked on some brilliant and well respected records. He had seen me play the previous year at a gig organised by Pledge Music where we briefly discussed the prospect of working together. Now, six months later, I sent him a message asking if he was still interested. He responded immediately and we agreed to meet within the week. I was nervous to play him my demos and felt insecure about my bass playing and the general production quality. I am definitely a vibe player and the often clinical nature of production is something that my temperament doesn't naturally gravitate towards!

A few days later I headed to Dean Street Studios, in London, to play Danton the tracks and was immediately drawn to his effervescent energy and mischievous sense of humor. His enthusiasm for the songs and the instrumentation laid my nerves to rest and he declared then and there that he wanted to produce the record. The excitement of potentially working with Danton was however slightly overshadowed by the fact I had no label to finance the making of a new record; both my previous albums had been funded through crowd funding campaigns. And so began the dilemma of how to cover the production costs.

Whilst the experience of crowd funding for Alive was incredible and ultimately I managed through the amazing support of all the pledgers to not only make the record, but collaborate with eleven artists each of whom created a unique piece of art in response to a song I had written. The final result was a beautiful book designed by Joantoni Seguí Morro, which included images of the artwork, the story behind the collaborations, the music itself and a DVD of films and artist interviews. There was video for each song on the record and visually this included footage of us recording at Hookend Studios edited to the footage of the relevant artist creating their piece of work; all pieced together by my dear friend Steve Teers.

The flip side of my crowd funding experience was that as an artist it is hard enough believing in yourself let alone asking other people to believe in something they have yet to hear and it took huge amounts of determination and courage to reach out and ask for support. In some cases the response was negative and often unpleasantly so, however thankfully this wasn't a common experience and in actual fact the crowd funding campaign was not only extremely nurturing but it enabled me to properly get to know many of the people that love my music. As an unsigned artist the words of encouragement that arrived daily really spurned me on, so thank you one and all. I was also acutely aware of how long it took to actually raise the money to make a record and how hard it was to balance crowd funding with running a label, managing a band, marketing a record, touring and most importantly recording the album itself and so I stalled.

After three months of resistance I finally resolved that if I wanted to make this record, a crowd funding campaign was the only way it was going to happen. Thankfully Mel Gow, the Valkyrie, had also entered my life. At my last UK gig before leaving for Germany in 2011, I played a headline show at the Union Chapel in Islington, supported by a soon to be discovered Jake Bugg. At the end of the gig I remember standing alone on the stage and saying thank you to everyone for their belief and support; there were many crowd funders in the audience. But I also remember saying that I had reached my limit and after ten years of being unmanaged, unsigned, running my own label, booking tours and shows, running the marketing and PR etc. I was running out of energy and I really needed some type of infrastructure if I was to carry on and not burn out. Mel was in the audience and approached me afterwards to say she wanted to be involved. She had no experience of managing an artist but was a creative soul, extremely competent and basically amazing. She was brilliant at online PR and website design and once I had chosen to do another campaign we decided that rather than running it on a third party site why not run it off my own website as I already had an existing crowd funding fan base. Having Mel's belief, encouragement and above all friendship at this time was invaluable as all the while I was just trusting I was making the right decisions.

In order to help raise the money I also took a marketing job for three months which reaffirmed that office life is not for me, but I did earn a good amount of money to add to the recording pot.

Once the campaign actually began everything escalated to a whole other level of intensity. In keeping with the decision to make this record truly personal, Danton suggested that as I had written and played all the instruments on the demos I should play them on the record. This was another step into the unknown for me, and the prospect of going into the studio alone to record without the support of my previous Alive and Libellus band mates (Jason Hart, Tom Robertson (Robbo) and Jo Quail), was daunting to say the least. I would have to deliver not only strong vocal performances but also nail all the bass, piano and guitar parts.

By December 2012, I was totally overstretched. Exhausted from working full time, running the campaign and trying to get the songs together I went down with a horrible kidney infection. Whilst the Banshee was in my sights it was clear that there was still a great gulf between myself and my muse.

After a ten day break it was time to begin and so on 7th January I travelled with Danton and Marta (our sound engineer) to Osea Island, a small island in Essex where you can rent holiday cottages. We had decided that as I was playing everything bar the drums, recording at Danton's studio in Central London would not be the best idea. I find London overwhelming at the best of times, but the thought of 3 weeks of 16-hour days surrounded by city chaos felt like a bad idea. I knew that I would need quiet to focus my mind and deliver all the parts without the distraction of wandering into a late night bar after a long day! Plus we were recording at a time of year when studios are normally fairly empty so I hoped we would be able to get a good price, which we did.

There is a main residential studio on Osea, but we only needed a small studio set up, so chose instead a small cottage with a writing studio next door. We set up to record and then over the coming weeks took turns to go down with the flu. This was January and there was thick snow on the ground and somehow we managed to break the boiler nearly everyday. Nevertheless, the vibe was great. There was just me, Danton and Marta for the most part, with Ben arriving towards the end. John Blease arrived in the second week to lay down the drum parts. Important to mention he arrived on crutches having fallen off a wall and damaging his ankle; not ideal but John, ever the stoic Scotsman, was not to be perturbed and recorded all his drum and percussion parts in two days amidst much banter and laughter. Incredible. Thirteen songs bosh! No faffing about. What a legend.

The cottage itself was cozy but there was enough room to have your own space and both the studio and surroundings were inspiring and we soon found a good balance of recording, exploring outside, red wine, late night editing sessions and laughter; fears of entering a 'Shining' esc scenario thankfully never arose. We were three eccentric people thrown into an intense experience that could have gone very wrong but thankfully didn't and we created a record that we are all very proud of. Marta and Danton did actually have a few days off the Island but I was there for three weeks and completely fell in love with the isolation and the beauty of being surrounded just by nature.

On the crowd-funding front I was still a fair way off reaching my target, and the flu was happily grating my vocal chords so in between recording the instrumental parts, I was frantically necking throat remedies and writing emails to as many supporters as I could. I had also begun applying for credit cards. I had never had one before, but this felt worthy just in case I didn't reach my target.

The next part of the puzzle was deciding who would master the record. Mastering like mixing, I think, can really make or break an album, so it was important we use someone that Danton trusted. Mastering an album basically means balancing the dynamics of the songs with each other so there is a uniformity when the record is listened to as whole. When we returned to London, Danton introduced me to his long-term collaborator Pete Maher. Pete has worked on some great records so when he wrote back saying he loved the album and would like to master it I was, as you can imagine, very happy!

By March 2013 the record was mixed and mastered and ready for the next step. This allowed me the space to begin thinking about how I wanted to present it. I knew that as with my previous albums I would create a book but I wanted to simplify everything. With Libellus, my first album, I had chosen a photograph, a piece of prose and a painting to represent each song. For Alive, as mentioned previously, I collaborated with eleven different artists, each from a different medium. The result was a book filled with the most incredibly diverse collection of artwork. With this album, The Banshee And The Moon, I wanted to strip it all back, keep it clear and simple and I wanted to make sure that nothing detracted from the music.

During this time I also made another radical decision. If I wasn't living in Berlin then I didn't want to be in the outskirts of another city. Inspired from recording on Osea and the peacefulness of living surrounded by nature, Ben and I chose to move from the outskirts of Bristol to Devon to a small cottage in the base of a river meadow next to a large flowing river and a beautiful oak forest. Once again I just trusted my intuition that this was the right thing to do. I would be moving even further from my existing Berlin and London musical community, but I had burnt out and needed to rebuild my energy.

Once in Devon it definitely took time to adjust. Berlin and the community of musical friends and creative mayhem that inspired me were still in the forefront of my mind but I knew that if I wanted music to remain a part

Photograph by Paris Ackrill

of my life and if I wanted to release this album, I needed to break the destructive pattern of pushing myself too far.

It didn't take long to adjust and after about a month of living in Devon I was walking along the river when my eyes opened; I saw inspiration all around and knew what my next step would be. I wanted a black and white landscape image for each of the songs on the album and, in order to complete the concept of the solitary artist, I wanted to be the muse of each image. Not in some egocentric way, I could be just a distant figure in the background, a blur on the horizon. All that mattered was that there would be just the photographer and me telling the songs stories thus unifying the artwork.

In April 2013 I began this project by working with Japanese photographer Akio Fukushima. Akio came to Devon after meeting me only once in London and we spent two days exploring the land, rivers and sea around my home. The cover photo was shot then; it was freezing but I suddenly had this urge to walk into the river, I felt the Banshee's strength growing within me and as I waded through the icy water, staff in hand, I was in someway cleansing all that had been. A clear determination began to take hold and I became very aware of what I needed and what I didn't need in my life.

In June, as the summer sun drenched the meadows around the house Ben took a series of photos. The first one on a balmy afternoon, as I spun and ran around the fields, feeling the wildness of life fill my bones. This image was paired with Run Let The River Run, the song I had written for Ben whilst visiting him in the Himalayas. The second, taken during the late summer as I sat by the river watching the full moon rise above the waters, was paired with Hear Me Now. Around this time my wonderful friend Maren and my musical brother in arms, Jim Kroft came to stay. I have known Jamie for nearly 20 years and during that time our musical paths have often interweaved. He has witnessed my journey first hand so it is apt that it was his photo of me leaping across the field, that I chose to represent the Banshee's metamorphosis.

There is one other image taken by Ben and that is for Trust In Me. I had written this song just as we had moved from our separate countries to Bristol. It was as you can imagine an enormous transition and there were many times when we both had to dig deep and trust in this seemingly radical decision. Shortly after writing the song, Ben took this photo of me and it felt right to include it now.

Later as summer was coming to a close photographer and pledger Serena Bolton came to Devon and we explored the moors and forests. I had a clear idea of what I wanted to capture and the fact that it involved being naked meant that I knew I had to feel totally at ease with the photographer. Serena's sister in law, Sophie, is one of my oldest and closest friends so there was already a huge amount of trust and understanding between us. This trust enabled us both to explore new boundaries and capture the images for Pieces and She Rises Up.

On 12th December 2013 I took the last of the images for this book with photographer Paris Ackrill in Richmond Park. Paris and I had met at a gig that November and I had shown her a copy of The Banshee And The Moon Vinyl I had created using Akio and Serena's images. Like me she was fascinated with moonlight and nature and so we decided to meet the following month to spend the day exploring and taking photos. The day we chose was one of those crystal clear wintry days when the sun shines and the crispness and beauty of the suns rays nourishes your soul. Later as the sun began to set, the mist began to rise creating an eerie stillness that set a beautiful scene for the images for Canary and Go My Way.

Before this story comes to a close there is one other strand that I would like to share with you. Whilst we were busy creating the images for the songs I was also on a mission to pay off the last of the album costs. Inspired by the private gigs I had done as part of the crowd-funding campaign, I decided to put a message on Facebook asking if anyone would be interested in hosting a living room gig. The response was incredible. And so, from September to December I set off around the UK and later to Germany performing in people's houses, gardens, a summerhouse, a warehouse, a castle basement, a cave, a theatre, a kitchen, the smallest living room I have ever seen, a wine cellar and many more extraordinary places. Some of the hosts were friends, some pledgers from the crowd-funding campaign, but many were fans of my music that I had never met in person. Each gig was roughly a 16-hour day. I would drive from Devon, in my little car jam packed full of equipment, arrive, set up, play for 2.5 hours, chat to everyone, and then pack down and drive to the next town. On average, I played 3 gigs a week but there were a few weeks when I played every night. It was without a doubt one of the most incredible experiences of my life. There is so little money in live performances, unless you are hugely well known, and in many UK venues, bands are only able to play for 1/2 hour.

These nights were run on donations, so listeners gave what they felt I deserved, plus I was able to play for a decent amount of time and properly get to know many, if not all the audience. The generosity of the hosts was unprecedented. Never before have I experienced such hospitality and kindness. Each night was full of laughter, delicious food and was truly inspiring, plus I paid off all of my debt. Thank you so much to everyone involved.

And so as 2014 dawns my third album and book, The Banshee And The Moon, goes to print, and as I sit here now I believe I have achieved what I set out to do. I wanted to capture who I am as an artist. I wanted the record itself to possess the energy I have as a performer, and with this book to create a body of work that reflects both who I am as an artist and my personal interpretation of the music. I am proud of what I have accomplished and truly thankful for all the support and belief that has helped make it possible. The journey of making this record has taken me across continents, into the very depths of my being and then out to connect with all those who joined the crowd-funding campaign. The often-daily words of encouragement have been incredible and it has been an honor experiencing all that has gone into making this record. My journey continues but for the first time in my life I feel a sense that I am becoming the person my muse inspired me to be.

Run Let The River Run

Written by Tallulah Rendall
Photograph by Ben Heron

My breath, naked steps, oh into your arms to fall
And these eyes, blue tides, so calm stay still for you

And I said, run let the river run my love
Run let the river run
Run let the river run my love
Let's dive to this rising sun

Run let the river run my love
Our freedom has just begun
Run let the river run my love
Let's dive to this rising sun

Your words, they live, with beauty's silence within
And I'll fly, I'll fly, my heart is soaring high, so high

Oh from the desert to the sky now
See storm clouds pass us by
Because I'll never be lost in the ocean with you
No I will never be lost, with you

Canary

Written by Tallulah Rendall
Photograph by Paris Ackrill

Bright spark in the darkness oh she fights for truth
Bright spark in the darkness fights the bare tree winter blues
Confusion in finding oh the light as she flickers to fly
Ferocious Canary redefines her battle cry

As she steps forth to fly her heart is in her eyes
With the braveness of her little light

She moves, she moves, she moves... Body is burning bright
She moves, she moves, she moves... Alive now into the night

She stands and faces now the noise with warrior wings
Unfurled to catch the slightest hope the sun might bring
Sadness it catches flight as morning frees the dawn
And out the darkness oh Canary she bursts forth

No more to whisper out into the night
No more to whisper out, she's alright

Pieces

Written by Tallulah Rendall
Photograph by Serena Bolton

Here a howling cry
I try to be brave but the tears are drowning the laugh inside
But I'll fight, with wilting strength
I fight to believe I can be much more than your words have said

Because all my life, all my time
Picking up the pieces, picking up the pieces
All my life, oh, I've been picking up the pieces of my life
And all my life, oh, I've been picking up the pieces

And the blame, you lay at my door
Sent a ripple down right to my core
And now this silence is all that I crave
I need to find my way to smile again

And in this time that I've been waiting
In this time been contemplating
How to find my way out
And in these days of illusion
The world comes fast and full of confusion
And the dreams I craved are to much to bare

She Rises Up

Written by Tallulah Rendall
Photograph by Serena Bolton

Born of beauty born of pain, rising high
Dancing on the mists of twilight
As she gallops wild and free across sun and moon and sea
She is boundless in her beauty

And the tendrils of her hair
White strands that seek and bare
The tide oh, she turns to see
The freedom in her veins
Untameable she claims the last laugh, as she believes

She rises up, she rises up, she rises up,
Cos she's woken to see her heart can believe in love
And her life it can be anything she wants
She rises up

As it dawns another day, setting moon guides her way
As she's turning now to slumber
And the hope you can inspire is burning higher
With the wisdom of your guidance

Shine On

Written by Tallulah Rendall
Photograph by Akio

Love let go, to the calling in your heart
The feelings you know, even though it seems hard

Let your love shine on
Let your love shine on
Let your love shine on
When there's nothing, oh there's nothing to loose
When there's nothing, oh there's nothing to loose

The moment awakes and the sadness flies away
He can catch your rolling tears and dry them away.

Let your love shine on
Let your love shine on
Let your love shine on
When there's nothing, oh there's nothing to loose
When there's nothing, oh there's nothing to loose
When there's nothing, oh there's nothing to loose

Go My Way

Written by Tallulah Rendall
Photograph by Paris Ackrill

Now that I am running free boundless steps childlike on the breeze
And friend watch as she is soaring now up to skies of snow, river running wild below
And I have found my way
Through clouds of grey

To stand alive, with my heart still in my sights
And I have fought the fight for many days and nights
And I can go my way now each and every day
Oh I can go my way now each and every day

Tales I've told will stay with me
But they are stories now and a person I don't need to be
And the ghosts drift up into the trees slowly disappear
And letting go I try to set them free
But as I lie awake with a smile on my face

I can stand alive, with my heart still in my sights
And I have fought the fight for many days and nights
And I can go my way now each and every day
Oh I can go my way now each and every day

Hear Me Now

Written by Tallulah Rendall
Photograph by Ben Heron

I am here, here for a moment
Whilst your hand holds, hands lie on my back
Warmth in the cold light, of a lamplight fades to long ago

And find me, an echo in a footprint
If you move to, move way to slow
And watching touches fall now, run away as, as they come and go

Cos I can't stop hear me now
Ohh I can't stop hear me now
Ohh I can't stop hear me now

And here take a lifeline
Through the new light, and through the snow
And broken things got mended, living childlike, childlike with new hopes

Cos I can't stop hear me now
Ohh I can't stop hear me now
Ohh I can't stop hear me now

The Banshee

Written by Tallulah Rendall
Photograph by Jim Kroft

She's standing in the Cauldron looking her in the eye
The birth of beauty broken forth and screaming up inside
And I can see the world. I can see her fate, all around in me
Suddenly broke forth, the Banshee broke to breathe

And so she stood and then she tiptoed to the sky, lightening caught her eye
And she stepped out from a shaded tree and took to flight to breathe she must leave tonight

Because her heart needs fire
She's gotta live life, live life
My heart needs fire
She's gotta live life, live life

She's grown so far the moon is looking up through stars to her heart tonight
And her eyes are bursting forth, burning free and there is nothing left to hide
I won't lie
She and I our hearts need fire

But now as the cold wind blows she walks alone
Howling wind has broken none of her bones

Land Away

Written by Tallulah Rendall
Photograph by Akio

In the quiet of silence my weary heart can breathe
Amidst the fallen sorrows, the rain among the leaves
And as the daylight passes the ink along the page
Another story lies hidden as it dies another day

In a land away, in a land away

And the voices drifting a mist among the trees
Shout out to hold the stories that should have been
But my steps grow tired as the shadows begin to hold
And the courage I once had doesn't stand now so bold

In a land away, in a land away

Land Away..
You can walk so far to be set free
You can walk far to be what you can be
You can walk so far see what you can see
You can walk so far just to be

Trust In Me

Written by Tallulah Rendall
Photograph by Ben Heron

I step towards where I belong
With each new day a new path is born
But oh my heart here at the start again
Oh my heart here at the start again

As I call to you
Another night falls and a new day is dawning too
Oh as I call to you
Trust in me as I trust in you.

But be patient now, be patient with me
What's easy for you is hard now for me
But I'm finding my way, getting right up again
But I'm finding my way oh back to you

Now alone in the silence
She's calling for guidance to breathe, to breathe
Now alone in the silence
She's calling for guidance to believe, to believe
Now alone in the silence
She's calling for guidance to see, to see
Because this is the closest I have ever been to me

Eyes

Written by Tallulah Rendall
Photograph by Akio

There's a beauty in this light, there's a beauty in your sigh
A beauty in the dark

But I am fighting through these days, in a silver lining haze, fragile but true
And there's a strength that sits unseen as we stand with truth beneath
A light it shines through
So when I fall I try to walk forwards
Oh when I fall I carry a hope to my bones

Cos these eyes have seen to many shadows to fall
Oh these eyes tell me oh you can carry it all
Oh these eyes believe they have felt it all
Oh so be kind, oh be kind, to these eyes

Bold fragility calm fires are burning free
With a body that spirals now
And as I'm carried forth I believe
I am where I am meant to be, so I trust this place in me.
But when I fall I try to walk forwards
Oh when I fall I carry a hope to my bones

Lost In The Moonlight

Written by Tallulah Rendall
Photograph by Ben Heron

Hearts are lost and found in the moonlight
As wide eyes they call through the street
And old friend you are here beside me now
As we walk a long way home

Saying over and over, and over, over and over again
That I got lost in the moonlight
On my way home
Oh I got lost in the moon
On my way home

I begin tall as a candle
As the room and the hour begin oh to spin
And I found you here lying beside me as over again I call your name and
Your saying over and over and over over and over again
That I got lost in the moonlight
On my way home
Oh I got lost in the moon
On my way home

The Banshee And The Moon

All songs written, performed and arranged by Tallulah Rendall

Recorded on Osea Island in a shed and a kitchen!

Vocals, guitar, piano, bass by Tallulah Rendall

Drums by John Blease

Sound Engineering by Marta Salogni

Sound Mixing by Danton Supple

Sound Mastering by Pete Maher

Production by Danton Supple

Photographers:

Akio www.akio-style.com

Serena Bolton www.serenabolton.com

Paris Ackrill www.parisackrill.com

Jim Kroft www.cargocollective.com/kroftfilms

Ben Heron www.biolaya.com

Book design by Joantoni Segui Morro

Photograph by Paris Ackrill

Thank you

so much to everyone who supported me both with words of encouragement and to all the generous believers who were part of the crowd-funding project. Thank you for pledging without having heard a note and trusting I would create something you would enjoy. Thank you to: my family, for your love and encouragement. To Mel Gow for your belief and incredible energy. To Danton, Marta & John, for your never-ending mischief, good vibes and a great fucking record!! To Marcin, for building my website for a pathetic amount of money. To all the Berliners for your friendship and inspiration. To Russell Swallow, Joanna Quail, Jason Hart, Robbo, Lucas Dietrich, Dan Telander and Jamie Croft, for your love and all the music. To the South West folks, Sophie Bolton, Graeme McCracken, Tom Hirons, Pete McCowen, Daverick Leggett, thank you for your wisdom and mischievous ways. To Rupert McKelvie, for my beautiful pedal boards. To Freq Scene for all your technological wizardry. To Joantoni, for your friendship, patience and graphic design skills. To Ulf Saupe, for creating the artwork for the Banshee Vinyl. To Ros Le Ber for helping create the image for Lost In The Moonlight. To Aurelia Bulter for the advice! To Pete at Genepool Records. To Isabel Balla, for helping to organize my chaos. Lastly, to the most wonderful of beings, Ben, thank you for standing by my side, picking me up when I fall and for letting me fly free. This record is for you all. You each stood by my side in your own way and with each hug, moment of shared laughter or word of guidance and friendship you helped me find the courage to make this record and find my way.

The 2012 Banshee And The Moon Crowd Funding Supporters: Alf Fairweather, Andrew Carr, Andrew Douglas, Andrew Thompson, Angela Woods, Anthony Marrian, Antony Sharman, Atlanta Kyte, Azim Noorani, Ben Heron, Benedict Jass, Beverly Smart, Candida Corcoran, Caroline & Jamie Heron, Chris Harris, Christian Tu, Christian Weber, Christopher Hook, Clare Dugdale, Colin Greenwood, Dallas Dacre Lacy, Dan Garber, David Cammell, David Jenkins, Dee Drummond, Derek Cattani, Ed Thaw, Elizabeth Dell, Emily Bliss, Evgeni Minchev, Frank Geretshauser, Fred Bartusch, Gareth Hayes, Gary Comerford, Gary Doyle, Gary Poturalski, Gavin Miller, George Piskov, Gill Aspel, Gordon Blackstock, Graham Bashford, Helen Holt, Ian & Michelle Bridger, Ian Spain, Ian Williams, Ishbel Macinnes-Manby, Izabella Kay, James Quiring, James Skinner, Jean-Pierre Du Plessis, Jeanette Mills, Jenny Slavova-Nowizki, Jerome Quiles, John Cole, John Elliott, John Fennel, John Hook, John Morris, John Rendall, Joshua Clement, Judi Etzin, Julian Simon, Justin Beaney, Katharine Hudson, Katja Kossakowski, Kenneth MacLeod, Kirk Goodman, Kjeld Thygesen, Lee Raudenbush, Leigh Hales, Leonora Oppenheim, Liz Brewer, Lloyd Ellis, Lorna May Wadsworth, Lukas Kroulik, Marcel Joppa, Marcin Zakaszewski, Mark Goodwin, Mark Lundie, Mark Simmons, Mark White, Martin Franke, Max Rendall, Mike Thom, Mrs. P Bouchot-Humbert, Muneer Hassan, Naomi Brewer, Nicholas & Annie Colquhoun-Denvers, Nigel Milne, Paul Mathews, Paul Shields, Pete Bryden, Peter Long, Peter May, Peter Wakeham, Petra Neuroth, Philip Anderson, Philip Bulcock, Pierre L'Allier, Prady Balan, Robert Bolton, Robin Anderson, Rodney Higgins, Rosalynd Brooks, Roy Campbell, Sally Farmiloe-Neville, Sarah Mills, Serena Bolton, Simon Fyffe, Sören Wolf, Steve Hughes, Stuart Guy, Susan McNeil, Tania Hitchins, Thorsten Baier, Tim Guy, Tim Joppien, Toby Abbott, Toby Cantlie, Tom & Kathrine Kitching, Tom Wyman, Toni Francis, Victoria & Ian Watson, Virginia DeMaria.

Photograph by Serena Bolton

"In silence the teachings are heard;
In stillness the world is transformed."
Lao Tse, Tao te Ching

www.TallulahRendall.com